daddy closet

poems by

CD Nelsen

Finishing Line Press
Georgetown, Kentucky

daddy closet

Copyright © 2018 by CD Nelsen
ISBN 978-1-63534-410-3 First Edition
All rights reserved under International and Pan-American Copyright Conventions.
No part of this book may be reproduced in any manner whatsoever without written permission from the publisher, except in the case of brief quotations embodied in critical articles and reviews.

ACKNOWLEDGMENTS

"A Clamshell Alliance," *Patchwork Farm Journal*.
"ghost of hollow/weenies past" (p.34), *Berkshire Review*, Volume 6, 1998.

Publisher: Leah Maines
Editor: Christen Kincaid
Cover Art: Melissa Barnes
Author Photo: Don Harris
Cover Design: Elizabeth Maines McCleavy

Printed in the USA on acid-free paper.
Order online: www.finishinglinepress.com
also available on amazon.com

Author inquiries and mail orders:
Finishing Line Press
P. O. Box 1626
Georgetown, Kentucky 40324
U. S. A.

Table of Contents

water whirling into 1

custodian 2

daddy closet 4

all I can eat Walt 6

Piper Cub 7

happening 8

ghost of hollow/weenies past 9

Macros on The Road 10

left coast 12

luminescence 13

wack bull out Coast Guard Beach 14

#notmypapa 15

A Clamshell Alliance 16

coyote valentine 18

dragon breath 20

alabaster safe 22

A C tree 23

Exhibit: Studies in Devotion 24

3 centuries: at least 6 devices 25

like I told the hawk 26

Certain Illusions 27

Tu B'Shevat chant 30

for D & Z & all my sistas

water whirling into

splash pulse against rocks below
WELCOME cascade for glass bottom boats
Spring Lake   San Marcos TX

can't see much under dirty glass over muddy water
back on shore, pay extra for well lit gals dressed as mermaids
half dancing as they suck on breathing tubes, shiny hair
glued down slick against wet, how slimy their skin must get

walking back to the parking lot, other side of sign says YALL COME
BACK NOW over that splash pulsing that glues my eyes to it until
my breath softens then I am dapple and rust in each rock, water
whirling into, out—beyond

too young to know I know where water over rocks can go

custodian

      ground usually baked to cracks by May
         one wet June: volunteer blooms riot in school field
unexpected transplants like most us Houston residents
        fluttering petals on undulating stems
                   under steamy bright blaze.

there where school will be
unless I can wish it away before fall
                 like bugs in flower heads
like rattlesnakes Daddy warns me about
    lurking in tall grass.

big bouquets for Sad Mommy everyday that June;
"don't pick so many, won't be seeds for more"
sweaty and dirty, clutch paintbrushes, blankets,
pink primrose, buttercups… more and more stems
                   to cut with safety scissors
                   hold tight in damp paper towels
                   thrust into pickle jars.
next morning, tractor mows it all down.

finally fall.
teachers' sweet jesus testifying voices
      flame in my ears.
our voices buzz in ragged lines
past fence, past unexpected wildflowers gone.

we march into cafetorium, salute the flag
fattest not mommy in brightest flower dress
turns out to be our principal.
she holds up the big flashcard: OBEDIENCE.
we must spell each letter out then say it three times
because we have been very very bad;
maybe why our teacher pinched us on our vaccinations,
    why she got fired that first fall.

more falls, more women not exactly mommies,
long days in hot Jesus haze.
lucky, just pretending to be good, finally chosen
to take the full basket down to Mr. Greenjeans.
if I give him my school photo, he will put it under
his desk glass with hundreds of others
      who smile up at me trapped there.

I promise to stand back safe from the incinerator
he lets me watch as he turns our messed-up papers into flame.

I won't give him my photo or ever obey again.
I know who mowed my flowers down.

daddy closet

Daddy had to retreat to this small hall closet outside my bedroom when Mother's beaded bags, high heels, cocktail dresses commandeered their bedroom walk-in. He triggers the bulb to magically light when the door opens, takes us to Hitchcock's *Psycho*, not realizing the b&w shower scene will haunt me in full color for decades.

I dance to the jukebox in the diner, last day of vacation. 2 of them stop bickering to watch other booths laugh and point at me tapping without tap shoes, swinging without hips like Shirley Temple: pageantry giddy as fake diamonds,
   bad politics.

"Need you a woman or a bottle to get through the night," Daddy confides in 6-year-old me. As confusing as lovey-dovey movies where they kisspuff cigarettes, look into each other's smoky eyes so well lit.

Mother shows us her reddened wrist, "Look what he did to me."
"Get a divorce, already," my no-it-all 10-year-old voice answers.

Mother takes back his diamond cocktail ring to pretend exchange for the one his business partner Frank gave her. How expensive these tiny Barbie outfits I don't want are, so intricate under cellophane, backed by cardboard.

I call Daddy to take 14-year-old me to the mall for a sweater:
"Where's your mother?"
"Out shopping in her mink stole again."

Life insurance reinstated right before Daddy's *accident*:
"He was chasing some big fish, didn't see the boat," Mother tries to soothe us.
"Of course, I called Frank, he's his business partner, a good family friend."

That's when I know who left the Chicken Delight containers still full of food in the backseat months earlier, her shrill "Don't touch that," higher than ever. Why she dropped us off at *Around the World in 80 Days* at the theatre across town, what we didn't want to see, where we'd never been before. Looking for what will never fit, I discover Lady Chatterley's paperback hidden under her bras & panties in the bottom drawer.

"I'm the world's oldest teenage werewolf," Daddy lied, he wasn't immortal like Elvis, even though he'd been shocked accidentally so many times working on his inventions they'd "never be able to fry me in the electric chair."

*No I won't do anything to get even with my mothe*r my mind screams at ghost him when I walk by his closet, magic bulb long ago burst. Sigmund's cigar chokes the air in there before fuming under the door. Bird beaks peck down from the ceiling, ghoulish cornfield orphans howl. Lady Madeline grins as her enlivened corpse falls on her haughty twin brother.

all I can eat Walt

15-year-old me wants men's wear
get sentenced to stationery & office supplies.

    & covering break for all I can eat Russell Stover candy counter
round display of stale hot nuts under heat lights
stuff myself sick before losing appetite like they knew I would.

distributive education: we little nuns of retailing get to skip high school
to work at Foley's because we aren't college material.

    & covering book department where *Listen to The Warm* gags me
Walt's *Leaves of Grass* gold-leafed, leather-bound, gets grabbed up
as grad gift by aunts and grannies, most with no idea what
beautiful subversion still lurks inside it a century later.

    & covering record department, blast *Are You Experienced*? Never
will be because they didn't assign me to men's wear. blast
Sunshine of Your Love, bring me some now, not this hot humid
Houston sun bearing down on poodle left in car with rolled up
windows until someone breaks glass to save her & her owners
threaten to sue him. want real warm unlistenably bright.

    guide diamond needle carefully into vinyl groove
so loud they make me turn experience sunshine down
while Whitman, one department over, offers his true body
electric
few, so gifted, will ever open or read.

Piper Cub

if we're chicks, where are our ½ wings to ½ fly
high enough to escape this persistent pecking
not need this improbable toy of metal and meters.

1 of 3 girls with Rich who's almost qualified for his pilot's license.
supposed to be tutoring each other in math instead
engine deafens, bumps make me burpy, velvet dark's barely lighted
by our beams.

below us, tiny stars twinkle on tiny poles, pearl strings of car beams,
under over overpasses, down offshoots of short drives with matchbox
ranches mushrooming. some windows lit blue, a pool like a teardrop
bright in one backyard. I point out mine as Rich starts our loop de loop.

tells us to check our seatbelts, hold on for dear life, then jokes about the
crash headline we could become.

happening

their groovy bounce announces
*we are pretending so hard not to look like
the toke parade that we give ourselves away*

vet Jer legless in his wheelchair
waits a beat before rolling out behind to share & deal
his way to earn some change, ride back to the nursing home

*don't you want somebody to walk me out in no morning dew
where you going with that gun love, love, love* from jukebox
loud enough to bring frats, nerds called brains back then,
hippies—others still beat, out from their separate corners
to whirl

ghost of hollow/weenies past

last bright leaves washed down
               that Columbus Day weekend
we stayed inside
   watched him play the game so
   he got the treat

even though she spoke up finally
          softly

outside
"no high-tech lynching,"
only the usual white handkerchief ghosts
    dangling from the usual trees

couldn't wear the costume that year:
              orange top over black tights
              broken masks over breasts
              empty Snickers and Juicy Fruit wrappers
                arranged leaflike over crotch
              plastic pumpkin upside down
                cracked open crowning me
              streamers of suckers like ammo
                down each arm

too many ghosts
too many hollow/weenies past

still

dangle

Macros on The Road

Michio and his macrobiotic devotees on an endless interstate
in the Midwest: starving.
Last riceballs and pressed salad gone hours ago.
"Stop there," Michio tells the driver and they all gasp.
A fast food joint. Ulysses and his warriors enter that Cyclopean cave,
no weapons against deadly whey and sheep meat.

The waitress looks at these curious arrivals—small Japanese man in a
worn black suit with white shirt and thin tie, some dressed like him,
the rest long-haired in jeans. Tells the cook, "Cult incoming."

All watch Michio peruse the menu. "Fruit pie and coffee" he orders.
"Fruit pie and coffee," all the
devotees order.
His daughter orders a salad, oil and vinegar on the side. Hot water for
twig teabag she pulls from her backpack.

As they eat their pie, she tentatively chews the riceball she didn't
eat earlier, tries not to notice the devotees trying not glare at her.
The only other woman there winks at her, remembering that early
morning when she, Aveline, Michio's wife; and their daughter fanned
the pressure-cooked rice so each kernel would cool right, wet their
hands to form the balls, pushed a finger inside each to make room
for *umeboshi* plum flesh picked off pits and the flowers they cut from
carrot moons. Some rolled in black gomashio, some in tan, the rest
with a nori strip across the middle.

Savoring the last riceball's taste along with the daughter actually
eating it, she remembers the first afternoon she met Aveline. She and
her mate arrived at a conference too late for dinner, having had little
breakfast, bought uneatable food from a peddler. Aveline took her
home and fed her, maybe guessing, maybe knowing she was newly
pregnant.

Aveline and Michio's daughter wants a chocolate shake but knows it will taste like creamy cardboard. Craves fries but thinks the duck or beef fat they are probably cooked in would sicken her unaccustomed tummy.

When she gets to the red *umeboshi* plum and carrot flower in the middle of her riceball, her father comes over and kisses her head. All the devotees smile and drink more water before they head down the road to California.

left coast

lawless lawyer lures me out to salt soaked OR edge, gets stormy, rescue my dog but not my stuff, broke not broken

rogue wave over my friend and dog on big rock below
really gone? my shock asks as water recedes, somehow
they still cling, soaked speechless
that rugged coast: the ultimate drama queen

you, shy MA guy, like my crepes, jump like a frog when I touch your shoulder, everyone laughs when I ask which way to the ocean, need a safe shortcut so no redneck will shoot me for trespassing

31 years later, we rent outermost house, remembering when it was 3rd in, float above sunset and serious surf, blowing sand cliff ever closer, search out your old cabin: a sunken-in garage, mine long ago reclaimed by trees

still hear sci fi creak of sawmill pulley bringing out dust, see smoke rise from sewers of Brookings, not shot, not wrecked when that serious gust blew the van across 101

luminescence

tear shaped, full belly focused,
must track down her mate's kidnappers
try to remain calm: protect their progeny within.

our collective breath held; former horrors pale—pebbles
before this boulder.

nacre, mother of pearl, more precious than any baroque gem on oil
prince's crown
                      than finest Akoya, South Sea or Tahitian
                      champagne/pastel/green/black/purple, pale
                      heirloom graduated strand on debutante neck.

despite Herculean efforts, he is killed medievally—can not say it or watch
videotape broadcast despite family pleas.

she grabs an AK 47 then returns it to the guard unused.
eye for eye of millennia pauses a moment,
easily sermonized, harder to practice.

nacre, mother of pearl, more precious than any baroque gem on an oil
prince's crown
                      than finest Akoya, South Sea or Tahitian
                      champagne/pastel/ green/black/purple,
                      pale moon glow.

you coat our worn world with abalone, redefine luminescence.

wack bull out Coast Guard Beach

shuttle bus driver says I shoulda called the rangers
got him put him in jail, at least given a big fine for
messing with wildlife like that other guy on another beach
        who hit one

you play you fish you swim through/against current finally rest
to gather energy to jump back in

thought he must be a vet checking on that huge old bull far from
the seal huddle, just wanted to pose, his big red face in front
then with the rest who couldn't leap back into the water
                              fast enough

in front of jet taking off, in lion's then tiger's mouths,
dangling off ice cliff—does thin herd but he's beaten the odds
not exploded by his own bomb, junk shot off by his semi automatic,
lovingly turned automatic

we boo as he grins, struts, phone playing badly amplified music
the wind mostly protects us from, much older up close
I lend the preg gal my binocs so she can see the whiskers, eyes and
wet gray fur as they climb back up

we ooh aah every time the huddle switches direction
each flipping over onto the next till he/she flips

#notmypapa

famously drunk on daiquiris in the Havana bar where
tourists fawn over you and your bronze bust, you whine
bout the burden a Nobel prize is, they call you old man at sea.

you weep: *why did I fuck around on my first wife,* while
skinnydipping with your third who wearily takes the gun away
again, so you can go write on that portable typewriter you can
barely stand up to anymore.

still reel with rocking motion of your short sentences, in gulf again,
in rented rowboat, sunburnt despite lotion, brother teases me:
can't even bait your own hook, how you gonna catch anything?
my bamboo pole gets more than their fiberglass rods.
daddy's rebuilt 10 hp motor sputters then dies.
he rows us back from too far out, waves almost scuttle
our insignificant craft.

some paid bigtime for your secretary to clean up their prose like that
would be the magic bullet.

will not pickle my brain until it and my wiener don't work (unable to
tolerate booze, lack other cumbersome equipment).

will not live to write, but, sometimes, while living, will write.

A Clamshell Alliance

Seabrook, New Hampshire 1999

My clamshell clamps shut
              so suddenly,
              so violently,
I fear/hope it may
  never/ever be pried open again
with the ambivalence
only a fake clamshell
in a miniature golf course can feel.

They've closed our whole thing down.
my burnt-out motor
will take at least a week to repair if
it can be repaired at all.

How sweet the trash heap beckons
       full of my old homies:
              signs for long gone taffy and egg creams,
              a neon bearded lady,
              cracked facefaded concrete strong men,
      all the beautifully evil obstacles whose edges can't be
                  filed smooth enough
                  for the fake protection
                  of this newest age.

Fresh plastic over my original wood,
green mildewed carpet where ocean floor should be,
no tiny schools of bright pencil fish,
just golf balls swim through my flapping halves
as that squeaky pulley opens and closes me 20 times an hour.

You'd think they'd name the frigging course after me, at least,
instead of that new electronic lobster
barely able to move his wimpy claws robotically.

I'm the one you must get your ball into
                              in that brief moment
                              I'm open.

No stars or octopi
never a diver hovering over me in wonder,
    her digital underwater camera trying to capture
    the painted whirl inside,
    the portal all must find a way through.

Instead, bored children batter me,
wedge their clubs in my opening for a wider shot,
first date teens play through my wavering shell distractedly,
weary adults along for the ride go through the motions
                              one more time.

Out front
coastal highway's so blighted with cars
a deadly amusement of its own.

Without the crowds, easy to reflect
on the constant bump and grind of it all
    how weather beaten I've become.

Still I dream of new paint and gears
    wonder if there really is an ocean two blocks away
    where delicately pink sisters
        burrow iridescent shells into bottom sand
        cooled by massaging fronds and grasses,
        hidden deep from the madding nuke that powers me.

coyote valentine

don't know we have a thing going on till search lights
out two patrol cars zigzaggy panic down both sides of the road
stopping right past our drive, your head pops up as you
try to leap away dragging broken legs behind: such power
such shattered grace that I almost forgive you
and your pack for the billy goat two doors down—his mate
cowering in shed after you took him, unable to bleat
knowing you would come back for her.

cop layered roly poly for 6-degree weather ambles up our snow blown path "just waiting to hear from the ACO." our 1/8 dingo barks his protest from the living room, we don't understand either.

"animal control officer. can't just shoot a coyote anymore."

"...then you'll put it out of its misery?" we ask or mean to ask.

he doesn't answer, walks back out to the cruiser, light still shining on the not exactly fleeing suspect, my valentine, who's managed to move back another 10 feet toward the frozen brook.

"just gonna leave it as long as it's not threatening you. let it crawl back into the woods. bullet could ricochet…"

wildboys musta heard it on the scanner or maybe one of em hit you, they emote excitedly as they aim their flashlights into the woods across the street. I call the cops back before they can find you. they rush away in their jeep, unsatisfied.

"you're not going out there," my mate ask/commands. 1/8 dingo eager to follow me out.

"didn't say I was." try to think of our hedge as a wildthing hospice, where chill, stupor, then letting go can proceed gently as it never does.

somehow, you make across the creek. Other paws track up, then away; how long did they listen for your howl before they knew?

3 days later, ACO lifts you up with gloves, so icy, you seem like a steamrollered coyotesickle from a Road Runner cartoon: the last indignity, my murderous love.

dragon breath

famous photographer asks mayor to let him burn down a house.
fire marshal eagerly offers him several.
he chooses the one my family members used to live in,
once white gray monstrosity near the mall: rickety, bad wiring, already condemned.

lovely glow inside windows bellows into dragon breath
beauty turns to ash, captured by cameras on cue: disheveled onlookers
only pretend to be tantalized/ traumatized/torn
some oblivious…

this is where a cousin woke up screaming from her nightmare fire at 2 AM, across town, block from city hall, her twin's bathroom candle burned down historic brickstone; that charred wall ripped open to reveal flowered wallpaper fragment, one china cup; my friend walked by, got upset, used that image in her poem.
I didn't want to tell her about the twins but did.

that brickstone rebuilt gloriously two blocks south of where the same photographer closed off traffic to capture beautiful actress in old car looking deserted, frail, in passenger seat, other door open, red and golden light below and beyond her, slick sidewalks, old storefronts above like tall goblins.

give book with photo of their former house burning down to family members. each looks half horrified, somewhat proud of her/his connection to dragon breath and famous posing, none mentions sad twins wailing,

all the times they complained to the landlord about the wiring,
                                        rotten stairs,
                                        peeling paint,

told each other what a death trap it was,
always worrying about the baby and the dogs—themselves—
every ash from anything they ever lit.

alabaster safe

don't tell the raped or murdered that without hate
there could be no love.

save that for the bejeweled toes of your beloved
alabaster safe breathing in conditioned air
                               above heated floors.

A C tree

Andrew Carnegie had this camperdown elm planted near his final home
sacred mother tree with such gnarled roots where he sought solace
after few appreciated all he'd done

not self seeding, had to be started by hand
hug it—feel sap flow through steel workers, libraries,
root up into you.

Exhibit: Studies in Devotion

that dumb curator put our paintings next to each other;
beautiful letters in lime and gold spell out *Studies in Devotion*
above us both mounted on this plum wall
slight pulse of security wire throbbing
            as if it could bridge centuries
                dividing us.

that ugly cherub in your painting's clouds glares over at me:
        floating with little wings that couldn't carry his weight
      above such a prim Madonna,
              her baby Jesus
              on bony knee,
              so cartoonishly adult
he could never suckle that discreetly bared breast.

ugly cherub who paid dearly to get his pseudo-pious puss
                          into your gilded frame.

ugly cherub staring at my suited love floating like a black snake over me
        as I hold my birthday flowers
                our world of eaten cake and tapestries
            spinning around us
        miraculously stilled.

soon
a microscopic speck from the ugly cherub's lower cheek
will show that he is part of a fake,
                a friend of the faker who painted him there.

the news may crumble this whole museum,
        topple a toxic mythology
           too many have been painted into.

3 centuries: at least 6 devices

pull strings,
tuck her pampered flesh into whalebone corset,
to serve, to tighten, to repudiate voluptuousness.

belly out backwoods spinster with cures
when corsets won't tighten,
I blow bass tones into empty moonshine jugs
between customers and witch-hunts.

1968:
hi fi diamond needle lowers down onto vinyl gingerly—
innagadadavida reverberates primally loud into our tween lobes
each supine body imprinting its own patch of orange shag carpet,
first clues of non-directed desire emerging.

20 years later:
nephew finds broken cassette;
we unravel its flimsy tape for blocks,
then loop it into Rasta curls,
taking turns on each head to amuse passing cars.

multi step odyssey to fuel this shiny turquoise clip:
your sweet inscription engraved too small to read along its edge.

I drive,
finally—my turn to talk;
look over midsentence,
you're checking your Blackberry.

later, you tap my appointment in
only then
almost glad I didn't throw it
                    you out the car window.

like I told the hawk

your majesty & terror seems fake like in
some video game or dystopian yah yah
till you make your grand entrance

STOP BELLYACHING MERE HUMAN, YOU
KNOW THE DEAL DESPITE FAIRYTALES&RELIGIONS,
REALLYGOODLOVE&DRUGS&FOOD&PETS&
EXOTICVACAS

BISH BASH BOOM WAAAAAH CRASH

haha dodge your mammoth wings swooping
down, nostrils & eyes ablaze, actual flames from your
open snout ready to roast me even before those sharp
claws grab my meat off its wagon, lift it skyward like
a mouse or vole morsel

not sorry bout that headconk from the mother tree reaching
out to shield me, sorry it only stunned you, that you scorched
it into ash, sigh

haha lifesucker, another spring has sprung & I
just climbed Monument Mountain in the rain &
finished the novel of 5 years & cleaned the garbage
down the road so

like I told the Northern Harrier
diving down on me at Canoe Meadows to belly
laughs from other birders, *not ready yet. give me
a few more years.*

Certain Illusions

Human beings are so frightened. Oh yeah.

You say we are talking together about why human beings throughout the world seek psychological security, but I'm only watching you, J. Kristnamurti, on a grainy video with echo-y sound from 1979. Your Hindu-twangish British accent so velvet beautiful even with coughs and throat clearing. How disciplined, yet relaxed, you sit.

Despite many, many revolutions…man has not been able to organize his society so that everybody could have enough food, clothes, and shelter. You suggest this need for physical security affects us psychologically.

Spoilt few wedged karmatically against the many poor, it injures all. You find my conclusion dangerous—a mindless echo back to centuries of my Judaic Christian roots even as I profess to reject them.

Why do we hold on? Is it we want to live with certain illusions in which we take delight? Never have two rhetorical questions answered each other so perfectly.

Why does the mind cling to a particular memory, to a particular experience, hold on to a belief which has lost all meaning, why? Early March: 8 more inches of snow. The puppy leapfrogs in and out of deep banks as I run along the shoveled path beside him. A little sun shines through; birds—not heard for months—chirp. My mind packs this bittersweet morsel away for future clinging.

MIND CLING FROM CHILDHOOD: My grandparents give me a little plastic boat with dropper topped bottle of vitamins cradled in its middle. To make it sweeter, a ten-dollar bill beckons from under the bottle. Greedily roaming the shelves, I lose the boat somewhere in the toy store. My mother lectures again: *"Someday, you'll put your child in the oven and the pie in the stroller."* Her words rise up 5 decades ago, cling wrapped, not just clinging.

Two trains go by, the first when you mention *envy being comparison, measurement from what I am to what you are,* judging it wrong the problem, not envy itself. Bring me a railcar big enough to haul away my steaming piles of green.

Morning and evening trains chugga-chug so loud they seem to run up the middle of my childhood bed a block away. Precursor of *sexual physical experiences but also so-called spiritual experiences which are far more dangerous.* Sometimes, JK, a train is just …a damsel tied to the rail, smiling Dudley Do-Right not coming to save her.

A plane that sounds like a dirty bomber approaches with *so you are struggling to move from the fact into non-fact,* your voice Socratically lulling, rubbing my tummy just enough despite the three tries it's taken me to get through your almost hour, *Are we meeting each other?* Hal the Computer took over our species in a movie, nukes threaten to mushroom. Our color chart of bright risks is finally discontinued. Virtual worlds require only touch to make all go whoosh.

You are so wizened, demure: huge calf eyes with long lashes.

Religious visions still *dangerous.* Now, really 32 years ago, you ask me, actually an audience probably half dead by now, to get rid not just of *certain illusions but the very idea of illusion itself.*

Why does the mind cling to a particular memory, to a particular experience, hold on to a belief which has lost all meaning? Because so much whirls around randomly, the wrong stuff clings, the right stuff lost.

MIND CLING FROM COLLEGE: vision of a gun shooting me dead as I try to grab the handle of my 1972 Pinto's front door. Daddy's raised voice telling me Houston is The Murder Capital of The Country. Violence rises with wet heat in crowded bars where men drool as women move like rattlesnakes…someone, maybe hired by the nuclear industry, murders Michael, an activist I know, outside La Mansion A Go Go—no longer about fake cowpokes on TV or drunken he-she brawls. I move up North, never have any children to misplace.

Are we done? Is this enough? You ask at the end of the 58-minute video, finally able to blow your nose and rest.

Powerful locomotives roar toward me, a plane flies overhead, I'm ready to leap tall buildings I must not imagine.

Tu B'Shevat chant

ROOTS
anchor fingers deep into earth
straw up nutrients
through
TRUNK
willowy
or elephantine boosting up angular network of BRANCHES
bare or lush with LEAVES/sometimes FLOWERS/ sometimes
even FRUIT

NORTHERN HARDWOODS: beech, birch & maple ablaze
SOUTHERN PINES: plantations with rattlesnakes on guard
TROPICAL RAIN FORESTS: real giants not houseplants
          iguanas too high to catch
          butterflies whirl thick as leaves
          baby anteaters suckle in underbrush
          rich yet fragile soil, how many more cures?
palms, gingko, weeping cherry
redwoods & dwarf ornamentals
lollipop shaped or fountain gushing
wind dispersed seeds of elm, ash & sycamore

DECIDUOUS: bare to lush then bare again
EVERGREEN: continually verdant

multifloored thangs sprung from tiny seeds reseeding
          claim sky while anchored deep in earth
SURVIVE dry/wet, cold/hot/wind/stillness/pestilence/maniac
poisoner/lover carving initials/hammock hook driven deep so
someone can sigh & nap in shade

leafbud then green umbrella then fire overcome by chill,
brown skeletons skitter & crunch to signal new leafbud again

ROOTS
anchor fingers deep into earth
straw up nutrients
through
TRUNK
willowy
or elephantine boosting up angular network of BRANCHES
bare or lush with LEAVES/sometimes FLOWERS/ sometimes
even FRUIT

CD (Cheryl Diane) Nelsen grew up in Houston TX then moved to Austin after graduating from University of Houston with a BA in English. In Austin, she booked cosmic cowboy bands at Moonhill Management and wrote PR for a jazz record company, Fable Records. She helped organize a co-op for musicians in the lobby of The Armadillo World Headquarters. CD wrote reviews for *The Austin Sun* and organized The Biggest Earful of Music Ever for $3 to raise moving costs for a food coop, Woody Hills, and participated in a comedy rock group called The Geranium Cabbages. Her sci-fi satire "Kisses Sweeter Than Cacti" was published in the glam rock magazine, *Creem*.

Out on the Oregon coast, she was published in *Total Abandon* and nominated for a Pushcart Prize. Her dog and she jumped in her beloved's bread truck converted into a camper and came to his native Berkshires in Western MA in 1977 where the couple still resides.

CD got two more degrees from State University of New York at Albany, SUNYA, an MA in English Education and a DA in writing, teaching writing and literature with an emphasis on feminist literary criticism. She taught at the secondary level for 25 years, mostly at Lee Middle and High School. Her 4 years as a college writing and literature teacher include SUNYA, Fisher Junior College and Berkshire Community College where she founded a labor movement for part-time teachers called Apartime. She has also led writing workshops at arts festivals and conferences including Focus on Women, D'Art Party, Women's Storytelling Conference, and The Dalton Cultural Fair. CD has participated in Made in The Berkshires 2 years, WORDXWORD story slams and other events, volunteered at Kripalu and Shakespeare & Company and as a literacy coach.